© Roberto Bruno 2024

No part of this publication may be reproduced without the written permission of the author.

DEDICATION

"I dedicate this book to all those who seek the courage to discover themselves, pursue their passions and build a career that makes them happy."

Introduction

Imagine waking up every morning with the desire to go to work, to feel fulfilled and to make a difference. Does it seem like a dream? Yet, it is possible. Each of us has hidden potential, talents and passions that are just waiting to be discovered. This ebook will take you on a journey of self-discovery, guiding you towards a career that you are passionate about and allows you to best express your abilities. help me develop this book

Pag. 6   **Chapter 1:** Who Are You Really?

Explore your hidden values, interests, and talents: Introduction to the concepts of personal values, interests, and talents. Explain how these elements influence career choices.

Self-awareness tests and exercises: Personality tests, reflection exercises and practical activities to help discover your strengths and weaknesses.

Pag 55   **Chapter 2:** The world of professions

Discover the endless possibilities that the world of work offers: Overview of the different industries and sectors. Career opportunities in each of them.

Market Trends and New Professions Analysis: Discussion of emerging trends in the labor market, such as digitalization, automation, and new professions that are emerging.

Pag. 62   **Chapter 3:** How to Find Your Passion

Practical strategies for identifying what you are truly passionate about: Techniques and methods for discovering your passions, such as journaling, mind mapping and informational interviews.

Visualization and Brainstorming Exercises: Guided activities to help readers imagine their ideal future and generate ideas for possible careers.

Pag. 68   **Chapter 4:** Build your ideal path

Define Your Short-Term and Long-Term Goals: Guide on How to Set SMART (Specific, Measurable, Achievable, Realistic, Time-Based) Goals.

Pag. 76   **Chapter 5:** Overcome Challenges and Achieve Success

Strategies for Managing Stress, Fear of Failure, and Procrastination: Stress management techniques, tips for dealing with the fear of failure, and methods for overcoming procrastination.

Winning Mindset to Achieve Your Goals: Discussion on the importance of having a positive and resilient mindset. Success stories and inspirational quotes.

Pag. 84   **Chapter 6:** Helpful Tools and Resources

A collection of resources to further your research and build your career: List of books, websites, online courses and tools useful for professional growth.

Pag. 92   **Chapter 7:** How to Create an Effective Resume

Step-by-step guide to writing a CV that will grab employers' attention.

Pag. 96   **Chapter 8:** How to Face a Job Interview

Practical tips for preparing for and successfully facing a job interview.

Pag. 118   **Chapter 9:** How to Manage Networking

Strategies for Building and Maintaining a Professional Network

Pag. 121   **Chapter 10:** How to Stay Motivated and Achieve Your Goals

Techniques to stay motivated and achieve your long-term goals.

Chapter 1: Who Are You Really?

Introduction

The journey to a career you are passionate about begins with knowing yourself. Often we find ourselves following paths that do not reflect our passions because we have not fully explored who we truly are. This chapter will guide you in discovering your hidden values, interests and talents, which are essential to choosing the career path that satisfies you the most.

1.1 *Explore your personal values*

Personal values are the deep-seated beliefs that guide our decisions and actions. Identifying your values will help you make career choices that reflect who you truly are.

Here are some examples of personal values and how they can influence career choices:

Examples of Personal Values

1. Autonomy

Description: You value the freedom to make decisions and work independently.

Career Influence: You may prefer a career ***entrepreneurial***, ***freelance*** or in roles that offer a lot of flexibility and autonomy, such as ***consultant*** or ***creative***.

2. Creativity

Description: You place great value on innovation and artistic expression.

Career Influence: You may feel most fulfilled in jobs such as design, writing, artist, advertising, or in fields that reward innovation and the creation of new ideas.

3. Stability

Description: You value security and predictability, both financially and professionally.

Career Influence: Careers with secure salaries and well-defined structures, such as government, banking, or established corporate jobs, may be a better fit for you.

4. Social contribution

Description: You want to make a difference in the world and help others.

Career Influence: You could look for jobs in the sector non-profit, education, healthcare, or social cause organizations, such as a social worker, doctor, or educator.

5. Innovation

Description: You are interested in pushing the limits of what is possible and experimenting with new solutions.

Career Influence: Roles in technology, research and development, or start-ups may be ideal, where innovation and cutting-edge technology are at the heart of operations.

6. Continuous learning

Description: The desire to grow, learn new skills and gain knowledge motivates you.

Career Influence: You may excel in academic, research roles, or in constantly evolving fields such as technology, where learning is a continuous requirement.

7. Adventure

Description: You seek excitement, new experiences and constant change.

Career Influence: Professions such as tour guide, reporter, travel photographer or jobs that involve frequent travel and daily novelties may appeal to you.

8. Personal relationships

Description: Put human connections and the importance of interpersonal relationships first.

Career Influence: Jobs that involve direct interaction with people, such as a psychologist, **counselor**.

What is a counselor?

*A **counselor** is a professional who, through active listening, empathy and specific techniques, helps people to **better understand themselves,** their **thoughts, emotions and behaviors.***

***Dealing with difficulties and challenges:** such as relationship problems, stress, anxiety, difficult decisions.*

***Developing personal resources:** to overcome obstacles and achieve your goals.*

***Improving the quality of your life:** through greater awareness and psychological well-being.*

In essence, the counselor is a guide who accompanies people on a path of personal growth.

What is the difference between a Counselor and a Psychologist?

Scope of intervention: *The psychologist deals with a wide range of mental disorders and can make diagnoses, while the counselor focuses mainly on supporting and accompanying people in difficult situations, without necessarily formulating a diagnosis.*

Training: *Both require specific training, but **psychologists** follow a **longer** and more in-depth course of study, which also qualifies them for psychotherapy.*

When to contact a counselor?

It can be helpful to consult a counselor in various situations, such as:

Relationship difficulties: *with your partner, family, friends or colleagues.*

Stress and anxiety: *related to work, studies or life events.*

Important decisions: *which require support to best orient oneself.*

Significant changes: *such as bereavement, separation, or relocation.*

Need to improve self-esteem and self-confidence.

9. Leadership

- **Description:** You are motivated by leading, inspiring, and influencing others.

- **Career influence:** You may aim for management roles, such as business executive, project manager, or team leader, where you make important decisions and direct a group of people.

10. Work-life balance

- **Description:** You are looking for a balance between work and personal life, without sacrificing free time.

- **Career influence:** You may prefer jobs with flexible hours or a company culture that promotes employee well-being, such as remote work or part-time roles.

Every person has a unique set of values, and understanding them helps you build a career that gives you long-term satisfaction.

Activity: Write a list of things that are important to you in life (e.g., integrity, freedom, creativity) and think about how these values might influence your ideal job.

Examples of Values and Influences on the Ideal Workplace

1. *Integrity*
- *Description:* The importance of acting ethically and honestly.
- *Workplace Influence:* You may want to seek employment in an organization that promotes ethics and transparency, such as nonprofits, government institutions, or companies with strong ethical codes.

2. Freedom
- *Description:* Preference for flexibility and independence.
- *Work Influence:* Careers such as freelancing, entrepreneurship, or roles that offer flexible hours and the ability to work remotely may be ideal for you.

3. *Creativity*
- *Description:* The desire to express innovative and original ideas.
- *Influence on work:* Professions such as designer, writer, artist, or roles in advertising and marketing, where you can use and develop your creativity, may satisfy you.

4. Skills and Growth
- *Description:* The importance of acquiring new skills and growing professionally.

- *Workplace Influence:* Careers that offer opportunities for continuing education and professional development, such as roles in companies with training programs or in research and development, may be appropriate.

5. Social Responsibility

- *Description:* A commitment to making a difference in the community or globally.

- *Influence on work:* Roles in non-profit organizations, in the public health sector or in companies with a strong commitment towards sustainability and social responsibility could be satisfying.

6. Stability and Security

- *Description:* Looking for a stable and secure work environment.

- *Workplace Influence:* Careers in established sectors such as government, finance, or large companies with workplace safety policies may be more suitable.

7. Collaboration and Teamwork

- *Description:* The value of cooperation and teamwork.

- *Influence on work:* Roles that involve working in a team, such as project manager, team coordinator, or roles in a collaborative business environment, may meet this need.

8. Innovation

- *Description:* The drive towards change and novelty.

- *Influence on work:* Working in startups, cutting-edge technology sectors, or companies that encourage experimentation and finding new solutions can be very rewarding.

9. Well-being and Quality of Life
- *Description:* The importance of a healthy work-life balance.
- *Influence on work:* Careers that offer flexible hours, remote work options, and an environment that supports employee well-being may be preferable.

10. Leadership and Influence
- *Description:* The desire to lead and inspire others.
- *Influence at work:* Management roles, such as manager, supervisor, or project leader, where you can influence and guide a team toward common goals, may be ideal.

Activity: Reflecting on Your Values

1. *List of Values:* Write a list of values that are important to you. For example: integrity, freedom, creativity, social responsibility.

2. *Reflection:* For each value, reflect on how it might influence your career choice.

Ask yourself:

- *How can I find a job that reflects these values?*
- *Which sectors or professional roles are most aligned with these values?*
- *How do these values influence my work preferences and career expectations?*

3. *Application Example:* Imagine an ideal workday that embodies your core values and write a brief description of what that might look like. This exercise will help you visualize the type of career that best reflects who you are.

1.2 Discover your interests

Interests are what excites and motivates you. They are often indicators of career areas where you might excel and find fulfillment.

Activity: *Answer these questions* :
- *What activities make you lose track of time?*
- *What do you like to talk or read about in your free time?*
- *In which areas do you feel most involved or motivated?*

1.3 Identify your hidden talents

Each of us has natural talents that, if discovered and cultivated, can become the strength of one's career.

Your talents may not be immediately obvious, but by reflecting on what you do you may easily be able to identify them.

Activity:
- Ask people close to you what abilities they see in you.
- Remember times when you received compliments for a job well done.

- Make a list of skills or abilities that come naturally to you, such as *problem solving,* creativity, or organization.

1.4 Tests and exercises for self-awareness
1. *Personality Test*
MBTI (Myers-Briggs Type Indicator) test
- *Description:* The **MBTI** is a tool that identifies the reader's personality type based on four pairs of preferences: *Extroversion vs. Introversion, Sensing vs. Intuition, Thinking vs. Feeling, and Judgment vs. Perception.*

- **Exercise: Overview of the 16 MBTI Personality Types**
The *Myers-Briggs Type Indicator (MBTI)* classifies people into 16 personality types by combining four pairs of preferences:
1. Extroversion (E) vs. Introversion (I)
- *Extroversion (E):* Prefers social interaction and outside activity. Tends to feel energetic when around other people.
- *Introversion (I):* Prefers reflection and solitary activities. Tends to feel recharged after time spent alone.
2. Sensation (S) vs. Intuition (N)
- *Sensation (S):* Focuses on concrete and detailed information, preferring concrete facts and experiences.

- *Intuition (N):* Focuses on ideas, concepts, and future possibilities, preferring to think in terms of big picture ideas and intuitions.

3. **Thinking (T) vs. Feeling (F)**

- *Thought (T):* Prefers to make decisions based on logic and objective analysis.

- *Feeling (F):* Prefers to make decisions based on personal values and impact on others.

4. **Judgment (J) vs. Perception (P)**

- *Judgment (J):* Prefers an organized and planned approach. Tends to prefer clarity and structure.

- *Perception (P):* Prefers a flexible and spontaneous approach. Tends to keep options open and adapt to circumstances.

Combining these preferences, we get 16 personality types:

1. **ISTJ (Introversion, Sensing, Thinking, Judging)**
- *Features:* Reliable, organized, practical .
- *Ideal Professions:* Accountant, engineer, administrator.

2. **ISFJ (Introversion, Sensing, Feeling, Judging)**
- *Characteristics:* Attentive to detail, protective, altruistic.
- *Ideal Professions:* Nurse, teacher, social worker.

3. **INFJ (Introversion, Intuition, Feeling, Judgment)**
- *Characteristics:* Idealists, empaths, visionaries.

- *Ideal Professions:* Psychologist, consultant, writer.

4. INTJ (Introversion, Intuition, Thinking, Judgment)

- *Characteristics:* Strategic, independent, determined.
- **Ideal Professions:** Scientist, analyst, planner.

5. ISTP (Introversion, Sensing, Thinking, Perceiving)

- *Features:* Practical, adaptable, problem-solving.
- *Ideal Professions:* Mechanic, detective, engineer.

6. ISFP (Introversion, Sensing, Feeling, Perceiving)

- *Characteristics:* Creative, sensitive, spontaneous.
- *Ideal Professions:* Artist, designer, social worker.

7. INFP (Introversion, Intuition, Feeling, Perception)

- *Characteristics:* Idealistic, thoughtful, empathetic.
- *Ideal Professions:* Writer, therapist, educator.

8. INTP (Introversion, Intuition, Thinking, Perception)

- *Characteristics:* Analytical, curious, independent.
- *Ideal Professions:* Researcher, programmer, philosopher.

9. ESTP (Extroversion, Sensing, Thinking, Perceiving)

- *Characteristics:* Adventurous, practical, energetic.
- *Ideal Professions:* Salesman, entrepreneur, athlete.

10. ESFP (Extroversion, Sensing, Feeling, Perceiving)

- *Characteristics:* Enthusiastic, sociable, practical.
- *Ideal Professions:* Actor, teacher, event organizer.

11. ENFP (Extroversion, Intuition, Feeling, Perceiving)

- *Characteristics:* Creative, enthusiastic, inspiring.

- *Ideal Professions:* Consultant, marketing, coach.

12. ENTP (Extroversion, Intuition, Thinking, Perception)

- *Characteristics:* Innovative, witty, sociable.

- *Ideal Professions:* Entrepreneur, lawyer, writer.

13. ESTJ (Extroversion, Sensing, Thinking, Judging)

- *Characteristics:* Organized, decisive, practical.

- *Ideal Professions:* Manager, military officer, administrator.

14. ESFJ (Extroversion, Sensing, Feeling, Judging)

- *Characteristics:* Sociable, altruistic, organized.

- *Ideal Professions:* Teacher, coordinator, social worker.

15. ENFJ (Extroversion, Intuition, Feeling, Judging)

- *Characteristics:* Empathetic, natural leaders, inspirational.

- *Ideal Professions:* Coach, consultant, manager.

16. ENTJ (Extroversion, Intuition, Thinking, Judging)

- *Characteristics:* Determined, strategic, leader.

- *Ideal Professions:* CEO, manager, strategic consultant.

How Results Can Influence Career Choices

- *ISTJ and ESTJ:* Tend to prefer well-structured and organized work environments, such as administrative or management roles. They may excel in careers that require attention to detail and reliability.

- *ISFJ and ESFJ:* They are attracted to professions that involve interacting with and supporting others, such as health care, education, or social services.

- *INFJ and ENFJ:* Seek careers that allow them to make a significant difference in the lives of others, such as counselors, educators, or community project leaders.

- *INTJ and ENTJ:* They prefer roles that require strategy, planning and leadership, such as managers, entrepreneurs or strategic analysts.

- *ISTP and ESTP:* They are well suited to careers that require hands-on problem solving and dynamism, such as engineering, sales, or technical roles.

- *ISFP and ESFP:* Excel in creative and social careers, such as artists, designers, or event planners.

- *INFP and ENFP:* Find satisfaction in professions that allow creative expression and interaction with others, such as writers, artists, or counselors.

- *INTP and ENTP:* They are attracted to careers that stimulate curiosity and innovation, such as research, technology development, or entrepreneurship.

Questions to Identify Your Personality Type:
1. *When you need to recover energy, what do you prefer to do?*
- *Socializing with others (Extroversion)*

- Spending time alone (Introversion)

2. When you face a problem, you prefer to focus on:
- Concrete facts and details (Feeling)
- Ideas and future possibilities (Intuition)

3. When making decisions, you are more oriented towards:
- Logic and objective analysis (Thought)
- Emotions and personal values (Feeling)

4. How do you prefer to organize your work?
- With a well-defined plan and clear deadlines (Judgement)
- With flexibility and openness to new opportunities (Perception)

5. When working on a project, you feel more motivated by:
- Well-defined structures and procedures (Judgement)
- Freedom and autonomy (Perception)

6. When solving problems, you prefer:
- Practical and proven methods (Sensation)
- New ideas and creative approaches (Intuition)

7. You feel more comfortable with:

- *Detailed and technical discussions (Thought)*
- *Considerations on how decisions affect people (Feeling)*

8. When you have a choice to make, you tend to:
- *Plan and take advance decisions (Judgment)*
- *Wait and adapt to circumstances (Perception)*

Big Five Test

- *Description:* The test of the **Big Five** measures five main personality traits: **Openness to experience, Conscientiousness, Extraversion, Agreeableness, and Neuroticism.**
- *Exercise* : Description of Traits and Their Impact on Work
Here is an overview of the four main traits of the *MBTI* and how they influence the way a person works and interacts in the professional context:

1. *Extroversion (E) vs. Introversion (I)*
- **Extroversion (E):**
- *Description:* Extroverts tend to feel energetic and satisfied when they are surrounded by other people. They prefer frequent social interactions and draw inspiration from their external environment.

- ***Professional Impact:*** They prefer jobs that involve teams and frequent interactions, such as sales, management, or leadership roles. They can excel in fast-paced, high-energy environments.

- **Introversion (I):**

- ***Description:*** Introverts feel recharged by spending time alone and reflecting internally. They prefer quieter, less chaotic work environments.

- ***Professional Impact:*** They tend to excel in roles that require concentration and solitary reflection, such as research, analysis, or writing. They may prefer to work in more private and organized environments.

2. *Sensation (S) vs. Intuition (N)*

- **Sensation (S):**

- ***Description:*** People who prefer Sensation tend to focus on concrete details and practical information. They concentrate on the present and the real facts.

- ***Professional Impact:*** They prefer tasks that require precision and attention to detail, such as accounting, resource management, or applied technology. They are suited to roles that require a systematic approach.

- **Intuition (N):**

- *Description:* Intuitive people focus on abstract concepts and future possibilities. They prefer to explore ideas and think in terms of big picture schemes.
- *Professional Impact:* They tend to excel in roles that require creativity and innovation, such as product development, strategy, or consulting. They may prefer dynamic and challenging work environments.

3. *Thinking (T) vs. Feeling (F)*
- **Thought (T):**
-*Description:* Thinking-oriented people make decisions based on logic and objective analysis. They evaluate situations critically and analytically.
- *Career Impact:* They prefer roles that require analytical skills and data-based decisions, such as engineering, finance, or consulting. They are suited to positions that require problem solving and rational thinking.
- **Feeling (F):**
- *Description:* Feeling-oriented people make decisions based on their personal values and the well-being of others. They tend to consider the impact of their decisions on others.
- *Career Impact:* They tend to excel in roles that require empathy and human interaction, such as customer service, human

resources, or education. They may prefer work environments that value support and collaboration.

4. *Judgment (J) vs. Perception (P)*

- Judgment (J)

- *Description:* People who prefer Judgment tend to plan and organize their activities. They prefer clear structures and deadlines.

- *Professional Impact:* They excel in roles that require time management and organization, such as project management, administration, or leadership roles. They may prefer well-structured work environments.

- Perception (P):

- *Description:* Perceiving people prefer flexibility and spontaneity. They tend to keep options open and adapt to change.

- *Professional Impact:* They tend to excel in roles that require adaptability and real-time problem solving, such as consulting, sales, or creative roles. They may prefer dynamic, fluid work environments.

Self-Assessment Test Based on Likert Scale

Here's a short test you can use to self-assess each trait on a scale **Likert** from 1 to 5, where 1 indicates " ***Strongly disagree" and 5 indicates "Strongly agree".***

1. Extroversion (E) vs. Introversion (I)

I feel energetic when I interact with groups of people.

- *1 - Strongly disagree*
- *2 - Disagreement*
- *3 - Neutral*
- *4 - Agreed*
- *5 - Strongly agree*

I prefer to work alone rather than in a group.

- *1 - Strongly disagree*
- *2 - Disagreement*
- *3 - Neutral*
- *4 - Agreed*
- *5 - Strongly agree*

2. Sensation (S) vs. Intuition (N)

I focus more on concrete details rather than concepts abstract.

- *1 - Strongly disagree*
- *2 - Disagreement*
- *3 - Neutral*
- *4 - Agreed*
- *5 - Strongly agree*

I like to think in terms of big picture schemes and future possibilities.
- *1 - Strongly disagree*
- *2 - Disagreement*
- *3 - Neutral*
- *4 - Agreed*
- *5 - Strongly agree*

3. Thinking (T) vs. Feeling (F)

I make decisions based on logic and objective data.
- *1 - Strongly disagree*
- *2 - Disagreement*
- *3 - Neutral*
- *4 - Agreed*
- *5 - Strongly agree*

I consider the impact of my decisions on others before making a decision.
- *1 - Strongly disagree*
- *2 - Disagreement*
- *3 - Neutral*
- *4 - Agreed*
- *5 - Strongly agree*

4. Judgment (J) vs. Perception (P)

I like to have a clear plan and follow well-defined deadlines.

- 1 - Strongly disagree

- 2 - Disagreement

- 3 - Neutral

- 4 - Agreed

- 5 - Strongly agree

I prefer to keep my options open and adapt to changes.

- 1 - Strongly disagree

- 2 - Disagreement

- 3 - Neutral

- 4 - Agreed

- 5 - Strongly agree

This test will help you think about what traits might influence your professional behavior and work preferences.

2. Reflection Exercises

Self-Awareness Journal **Exercise**

- Description: Keeping a journal can help you reflect on everyday experiences and how they influence your self-awareness.

Exercise: *Diary of Emotions and Experiences*

Objective: Write a daily journal for two weeks to explore what makes you happy, frustrated, or satisfied. This exercise will help you identify patterns and personal preferences that can guide you toward a career you are passionate about.

Exercise Instructions:

1. *Preparing the Diary:*
- ***Necessary Material:*** A notebook or note-taking app on your smartphone or computer.
- ***Setup:*** Spend 10-15 minutes at the end of each day to complete your journal. Try to do it at the same time each day to create a routine.

2. Structure of the Diary:
- *Date:* Start each entry with the date.
- *Moments of Happiness:* Briefly describe an event or activity that made you happy or satisfied during the day. What contributed to this feeling? Who was there? How did you feel?
- *Moments of Frustration:* Describe an event or situation that frustrated or disappointed you. What happened? How did you react? What could you have done differently?

- ***Reflections:*** At the end of each entry, write a reflection on how the event or activity affected your day and what you learned about yourself. It can be helpful to ask questions like:

- *"What made me feel satisfied today?"*
- *"What caused me stress or frustration?"*
- *"What can I do to increase moments of happiness and reduce moments of frustration?"*

3. Weekly Analysis:

- At the end of each week, review your journal and look for patterns in your feelings. Ask yourself:

- *"What activities or situations tend to make me feel happier or more satisfied?"*
- *"What factors are common in moments of frustration?"*
- *"Are there any recurring themes that emerge from my writings?"*

4. Final Reflection:

- After two weeks, reflect on what you have learned from your observations. Consider:

- *"What have these two weeks taught me about what motivates and rewards me?"*
- *"How can I apply these insights in my career or professional choices?"*
- *"Are there aspects of my current professional life that I can change to improve my well-being and satisfaction?"*

Journal Entry Example:

- *Date:* **March 18, 2024**

- *Moments of Happiness:* Today I felt happy while working on a group project. Collaboration with colleagues was stimulating and we achieved a great result. I really enjoyed sharing ideas and solutions.

- *Moments of Frustration:* I found it frustrating to have to deal with a tight deadline for a report. I had little time to complete the work and felt overwhelmed.

- *Reflections:* I realize that I find teamwork and collaboration very rewarding, while tight deadlines and individual work make me uncomfortable. Perhaps I should look for job opportunities that allow me to work in groups more often and manage my time better.

This exercise will help you gain a clearer vision of what motivates and rewards you, facilitating a career choice that is more aligned with your true interests and values.

Exercise of the 3 Qualities

- *Description:* Identify three main qualities that you recognize in yourself and reflect on how these influence your working life

Exercise: *Identify and Utilize Your Strongest Qualities*

Objective: Reflect on your strongest qualities and how they can influence your career choice. This exercise will help you better understand your skills and how to apply them in your career.

Exercise Instructions

1. ***Identify Your Strongest Qualities:***

- *Step 1:* Make a list of the three qualities that you consider to be your strongest. These can include traits such as creativity, leadership, resilience, problem-solving, etc.

- *Step 2:* For each quality, write a short description of what it means to you and why you feel it is one of your strongest qualities.

2. Describe the Situations:

- *Step 1:* For each of the three qualities identified, reflect on specific situations in which this quality manifested itself. These could be work experiences, personal projects, or even everyday situations.

- *Step 2:* Describe each situation in detail. Answer questions like:

- *"In what context did this situation occur?"*

- *"What were the challenges or goals?"*

- *"How did you use this quality to deal with the situation?"*

- *"What was the result?"*

3. Career Reflection:

- *Step 1:* Consider how these qualities might influence your career choice. Think about how your ideal job might leverage these qualities.

- *Step 2:* Think about how these qualities can be an advantage in your future career opportunities. Ask yourself:

- *"In what types of roles or industries might these qualities be particularly valuable?"*

- *"How can I highlight these qualities on my resume, during an interview or in my daily work?"*

Example of Completing the Exercise:

1. *Quality: Creativity- Description:* I consider myself a creative person because I like finding innovative solutions to problems and thinking outside the box.

- *Situation:* During a marketing project for my company, I created an original advertising campaign that attracted customers' attention and increased sales by 20%. I used my creativity to develop unique and visually appealing concepts.

- *Career Reflection:* My creativity would be particularly useful in roles such as design, marketing or strategy consulting. I can look for opportunities that allow me to use and further develop this quality.

2. Quality: Leadership Skills

- **Description:** I have strong leadership skills, which allows me to guide and motivate teams towards common goals.
- **Situation:** As a team leader on a software development project, I coordinated the work of several team members, ensuring that everyone remained motivated and focused on the project goals. The project was completed successfully and ahead of schedule.
- **Career Reflection:** My leadership skills would be well utilized in management roles, such as a manager of project or department director. I should seek opportunities that allow me to lead and inspire others.

3. Quality: Problem Solving Ability

- **Description:** I am skilled at solving complex problems through critical analysis and generating practical solutions.
- **Situation:** During a crisis meeting with a customer, I quickly analyzed the technical issues and proposed a solution that effectively solved the problem, restoring the customer's trust and preventing further inconvenience.
- **Career Reflection:** My problem-solving skills could be valuable in roles that require strong critical analysis and decision-making, such as a consultant or analyst. I should look for roles that allow me to use this quality to address challenges and find solutions.

This exercise will help you focus on your main qualities and understand how they can guide your career choices.

3. Skills Assessment Exercises

Skills Matrix Exercise

- **Description:** Assess your skills and how they can be applied to different professional roles

Exercise: *Matrix of Professional Skills and Roles*

Objective: Create a matrix to map your core competencies and explore how they can be applied or improved in the job roles you are interested in. This exercise will help you identify areas where your skills can be an advantage and skills you may want to develop further.

Exercise Instructions:

1. Matrix Preparation:

- **Materials Required:** A sheet of paper or a digital document to create a matrix. You can use a spreadsheet for easier management.
- **Setting:** Draw a table with two main columns: one for your skills and one for the job roles you are interested in.

2. *Filling in the Matrix:*

- *Step 1:* List of Skills

- Write a list of your core competencies in the left column. Competencies may include, but are not limited to:

- *Communication*
- *Troubleshooting*
- *Technical skills (e.g. programming, data management)*
- *Leadership*
- *Ability to work in a team*
- *Creativity*
- *Organization*

- *Step 2: List of Job Roles*
- *In the right column, list the job roles or careers that interest you. Some examples could be: - Project Manager*
- *Data analyst*
- *Graphic designer*
- *Marketing Specialist*
- *Engineer*
- *Consultant*

3. Analysis and Reflection:

- *Step 1: Applying Skills to Roles*

- For each skill listed, think about how it can be applied in the different job roles you have identified. You can make notes next to each role to indicate how your skill is useful or necessary.

- **Example:**

- ***Communication:*** Essential for a Project Manager to coordinate the team and negotiate with clients. Also useful for a Marketing Specialist to create effective advertising campaigns.

-***Problem Solving*** Essential for a Data Analyst to solve complex problems and find insights in data. Also important for an Engineer to address and solve technical challenges.

- *Step 2: Identify Areas for Improvement*

- Identify skills that could be further developed to better suit the roles you are interested in. For example, if you are interested in a Graphic Designer role but do not have advanced skills in design software, this may be an area for improvement.

4. Final Reflection:

- *Reflect on how your skills align with the job roles you have chosen. Consider:*

- *"What skills are particularly in demand in the roles I am interested in?"*

- *"How can my skills give me a competitive advantage in these roles?"*

- *"What skills do I need to further develop to achieve my professional goals?"*

Matrix Example:

Skills	Professional Roles	Applications of Skills
Communication	Project Manager, Marketing Specialist	Coordination, negotiation, creation of advertising campaigns
Problem Solving	Data Analyst, Engineer	Solving complex problems, analyzing data, tackling technical challenges
Technical skills	Engineer, Graphic Designer graphic	Technical work, design, use of design software
Leadership	Project Manager, Consultant	Team leadership, project management, influencing customer decisions

This exercise will help you visualize how your skills can be used in the roles you are interested in and identify areas where you can improve.

Exercise: Personal SWOT Analysis

Description: SWOT analysis is a strategic tool that helps you assess your strengths, weaknesses, opportunities, and threats so you can gain a clear view of your resources and the challenges you may face. This exercise will guide you in reflecting on these aspects and planning how to best utilize your potential to achieve your professional and personal goals.

Exercise Instructions:

1. *Preparation of the SWOT Matrix:*

- *Necessary Material:* A sheet of paper or a digital document. You can use a spreadsheet for easier management.

- *Setting:* Draw a table divided into four sections: Strengths, Weaknesses, Opportunities and Threats. Each section represents one of the aspects of the SWOT analysis.

2. *Completion of the SWOT Matrix:*

- *Strengths:*

- *Step 1:* Reflect on your personal and professional strengths. What do you do well? What skills, resources, or qualities do you have that give you an edge?

- *Step 2:* Write these points in the "Strengths" section of the matrix. Examples might include specific skills, experiences, accolades, or positive character traits.

- *Example:* Many years of experience in project management, excellent communication skills, and strong problem-solving skills.

- *Weaknesses:*
- *Step 1:* Identify areas where you could improve. What are your weaknesses? What is holding you back from achieving your goals?
- *Step 2:* Write down these aspects in the "Weaknesses" section. They may include lack of experience in certain areas, insufficient skills, or personal challenges.
- *Example:* Lack of experience with recent technologies, difficulty managing time, and a tendency to procrastinate.

- *Opportunity:*
- *Step 1:* Consider the opportunities you can take advantage of to grow and improve. What market trends, changes, or resources can help you achieve your goals?
- *Step 2:* List these opportunities in the "Opportunities" section. This could include new trends in your industry, available training courses, or professional networks to explore.
- *Example:* Growing demand for digital skills, networking opportunities through industry events, and access to online refresher courses.

- *Threats:*
- *Step 1:* Identify threats or challenges that could hinder your progress. What external factors can negatively impact your path?

- *Step 2:* Write these threats in the "Threats" section. They may include adverse economic conditions, increasing competition, or regulatory changes in your field.

- *Example:* Economic instability of the sector, high competition for high-level positions, and rapid changes in the technologies used.

3. Reflection and Planning:

- *Step 1:* Examine your SWOT matrix and reflect on how you can use your strengths to address your weaknesses and exploit opportunities.

- *Step 2:* Think about strategies to mitigate threats. For example, you might look to acquire new skills to overcome weaknesses or prepare for growing competition.

SWOT Matrix Example:

Strengths

Many years of experience
in project management

Excellent communication skills

Strong problem-solving skills

Weaknesses

Lack of experience
in recent technologies

Difficulty in time management

Tendency towards procrastination

Opportunities

Growing demand for digital skills

Networking opportunities through
industry events

Access to online refresher courses

Threats

Economic instability of the sector

High competition for
high-level positions

Rapid Changes in Technologies

This exercise will help you better understand your resources and the challenges you face, facilitating strategic planning for your personal and professional development.

4. Visualization Exercises

Ideal Vision Exercise

Description: The Ideal Vision Exercise is an activity that helps you visualize the work and professional life that best reflects your values and desires. Imagining an ideal day at work will help you identify the key aspects of a fulfilling and motivating career, helping you make informed decisions about how to orient your career toward goals that you are truly passionate about.

Exercise Instructions:

1. *Preparation:*

- *Materials Required:* A notebook or digital document to jot down your thoughts.

- *Environment:* Find a quiet place where you can concentrate without distractions. It is helpful to dedicate at least 15-30 minutes to this exercise.

2. *Guided Imagery:*

- *Step 1:* Close your eyes and imagine waking up one day in your ideal life. Visualize your environment, your thoughts and your emotions.

- *Step 2:* Imagine starting your work day. What are the first things you do in the morning? How do you feel as you get ready for work?

3. *Detailed Description:*
- ***Step 3:*** Describe your ideal work day in detail:
- ***Activities:*** What exactly are you doing? What tasks and projects do you engage in? Are they creative, analytical, strategic, or practical activities?
- ***Environment:*** Where do you work? Is it a traditional office, a shared workspace, or perhaps a remote environment? How is your workspace furnished? Is there a particular feel or style that you favor?
- ***Colleagues:*** Who surrounds you? Do you work in a team, alone, or with a mentor? What are the characteristics of the people you work with?
- ***Interactions:*** Who do you interact with during the day? What are your professional relationships like? Do you lead meetings, work closely with clients, or participate in group brainstorming?
- ***Emotions:*** How do you feel during your ideal day? Are you satisfied, motivated, stimulated? What emotions predominate during work?

4. *Reflection:*
- ***Step 4:*** After describing your ideal day, reflect on the following:
- ***Alignment:*** How well do your current career or the career options you are considering align with this ideal vision?

- *Changes:* What could you change about your current situation to get closer to your ideal workday?
- *Goals:* What professional and personal goals can you set to build a career that reflects this vision?

5. *Notes and Planning:*

- *Step 5:* Write down your reflections and the insights you gained. Use this information to guide your future decisions, such as choosing a new job, upgrading your skills, or exploring new career opportunities.

This exercise will help you clarify what is truly important to you in a job and how you can structure your career to reflect those values and desires. If you need further guidance or clarification, I'm here to help!

Exercise: Mind Map of Passions and Interests

Description: Creating a mind map of your passions and interests is an exercise that will help you visualize and organize your personal inclinations and how they can translate into career opportunities. This approach allows you to creatively explore the connections between what you love to do and the careers that might fulfill those passions.

Exercise Instructions:

1. Preparation:

- *Materials needed:* A large sheet of paper or a digital mind mapping application (such as XMind, MindMeister or simply a drawing document).

- *Environment:* Find a quiet and stimulating environment where you can focus without distractions. Spend about 30-60 minutes on this exercise.

2. Creating the Mind Map:

- *Step 1: Start with the Center:*

- Write "My Passions and Interests" in the center of the paper or mind map. This will be your starting point.

- *Step 2: Identify Passions and Interests:*

- *List:* Think about the activities, topics and areas that you are most passionate about. These may include hobbies, subjects of study, skills, or aspects of your life that you find particularly rewarding.

- *Connections:* Draw branches from the center for each of your passions or interests. Label each branch with a specific area (e.g., "Art," "Technology," "Travel").

- *Step 3: Expand Connections:*

- *Subcategories:* For each main area, create sub-branches that represent more specific aspects or subcategories of your passions.

For example, under *"Technology"* you might have *"Software Development ," "Cybersecurity," or "Innovation ."*

- **Possible Careers:** Link each subcategory to possible careers or job roles that match that passion. Add these careers as third branches. For example, under *"Software Development"* you might have roles like *"Frontend Developer," "Software Engineer," or "Data Analyst."*

- *Step 4: Viewing Opportunities:*

- **Explore Connections:** See how your passions and interests connect to different career opportunities. Identify areas where there is a strong fit between what you love to do and the careers that appeal to you.

- **Prioritization:** Select the areas that seem most promising or that you are most attracted to and mark them in your mind map.

3. Reflection and Planning:

- *Step 5: Review Your Map:*

- **Analyses:** Analyze your mind map to identify any trends or connections you hadn't noticed before. Which career areas stand out as particularly attractive?

- **Growth Opportunities:** Consider how you can further develop your skills in the areas that interest you most. What steps can you take to enter these professions?

- *Step 6: Planning Next Actions:*

-Goals: Set concrete goals for exploring or entering the career fields you've identified. This may include seeking training, internships, or networking with industry professionals.

Mind Map Matrix

My Passions and Interests	Art	Technology	Trips
	Drawing	Software development	Adventures
	Painting	Frontend Developer	Culture
	Music	Software Engineer	
		Cybersecurity	
		Data Analyst	
		Tester	
		Innovation	

This exercise will help you connect your passions to career opportunities, clarifying which direction might be best for you.

Exercise 1: *Personal Values Test*

Description: This test will help you identify which values are most important to you and how these values can influence your career and personal choices. Rank the following values in order of importance to you, with 1 being the most important and 8 being the least important.

Instructions: Assign a score to each value and write down your answers. Use this ranking to reflect on how your priority values influence your career decisions and career preferences.

Values to be classified:
1. Success
2. Stability
3. Adventure
4. Connection
5. Personal growth
6. Security
7. Freedom
8. Innovation

Test Questions:
1. Success: How important is it for you to achieve significant results and recognition in your career and life?
2.Stability: How much do you value safety and predictability in your work environment and daily life?
3. Adventure: How important is it for you to face new challenges and live exciting and unpredictable experiences?

4. *Connection:* How important is it to you to build meaningful relationships and work in a collaborative, supportive environment?

5. *Personal growth:* How much do you want to develop your skills and continually learn new skills?

6. *Security:* How important is it for you to have a strong support network and a stable foundation in your professional and personal life?

7. *Freedom:* How much do you value the freedom to make independent decisions and have control over your actions and career?

8. *Innovation:* How important is it for you to work on innovative projects and contribute to significant changes and progress?

Exercise 2: *Personal SWOT*

Description: A personal SWOT analysis allows you to take stock of who you are, what you have available, and what challenges you may face. This reflection will help you better understand how to leverage your strengths and address your weaknesses to achieve your professional and personal goals.

Instructions: Complete the personal SWOT matrix by following the guiding questions. Reflecting on these areas will provide you with a clear view of your capabilities and areas for improvement.

Personal SWOT Matrix:

1. Forces:
- What are your main skills and abilities?
- What unique resources or advantages do you have available to you?
- What sets you apart from others in your professional field?

Examples of answers:
- Excellent communication skills
- Strong leadership
- Significant experience in a specific sector

2. Weaknesses:
- What are your main areas for improvement?
- What skills do you lack or what areas do you feel you struggle with?
- What could you improve to be more effective in your work?

Examples of answers:
- Tendency to procrastinate
- Lack of experience in new technologies
- Difficulty in teamwork

3. Opportunities:

- What trends or changes in your industry might offer new opportunities?

- Are there training courses, professional networks, or other resources you could leverage?

- How can you capitalize on your strengths to seize new opportunities?

Examples of answers:

- New technological trends in your field

- Professional development courses available

- Expanding your professional network through industry events

4. Threats:

What external factors might be hindering your success?

- Are there any changes in the job market or in your industry that could negatively affect you?

- What personal challenges might impede your progress?

Examples of answers:

- More and more qualified competitors

- Rapid changes in technology requiring continuous updates

- Personal situations that require attention and time

Conclusion:

Use the insights from your SWOT analysis and values test to make informed decisions about your career. Understanding your strengths and weaknesses, as well as opportunities and threats, will help you better orient your career toward a path that reflects your personal values and aspirations.

Chapter Conclusion:

In this chapter, we explored several tools and techniques for deepening self-awareness, a crucial step in choosing a career that not only reflects your personal inclinations, but also offers you long-term satisfaction and motivation.

You have learned:
- *Identification of Personal Values:* How your core values influence your career decisions and help you make choices that are in tune with who you truly are.

- *Self-Awareness Tests and Exercises:* Techniques such as the MBTI test and the emotion diary that allow you to discover and better understand your personal and professional characteristics.

- *Personal SWOT Analysis:* How to assess your strengths, weaknesses, opportunities and threats to gain a clear view of your potential and challenges.

- *Ideal Vision:* The importance of imagining an ideal workday to define the key aspects you want in your career.

- *Mind Map of Passions and Interests:* How to connect your passions to potential career opportunities, making visible connections between what you love to do and careers that might fulfill you.

Next Steps:

Now that you've explored these tools and reflected on yourself, it's time to put what you've learned into practice. Use this information to guide your career decisions and plan your next steps in your career. Consider the following tips for applying what you've learned:

1. *Develop an Action Plan:* Based on your values, strengths, and passions, create a detailed plan to pursue the careers that interest you. Set concrete and realistic goals to achieve these goals.

2. *Explore Opportunities:* Seek out opportunities for training, networking, and hands-on experience in the field that interests you. Talk to industry professionals, attend events, and continue to expand your knowledge.

3. *Reflect and Adapt:* Self-awareness is an ongoing process. Periodically, reflect back on what you've learned and how your career choices align with your ideal vision. Don't be afraid to adjust your path if necessary.

I encourage each of you to take the time to reflect on these findings and use them as a guide in building your a career that not only brings you professional success, but also enriches your personal life. Remember that the path to a fulfilling career is a combination of exploration, self-knowledge, and conscious action.

In the next chapter, we'll explore the world of careers and how to identify opportunities that align with your passions and skills. Continue following your journey of discovery and get ready to put the insights you've gained so far into action.

Chapter 2: The world of professions

Introduction

The world of work is a vast and ever-changing universe. Once you have identified your values, interests, and talents, it is essential to understand the infinite possibilities that different industries and sectors can offer. Choosing a career is no longer a matter of adapting to a pre-established path, but of finding the right field where you can best express your potential. In this chapter, we will explore the main professional areas and the opportunities they offer, as well as discuss emerging trends and new professions that are growing thanks to transformations such as digitalization and automation.

2.1 *Discover the infinite possibilities of the world of work*

The world of careers is extremely diverse, with opportunities spanning traditional and innovative sectors. The key is to understand your options, explore industries that align with your interests, and identify the type of environment you would like to work in. Here is an overview of the main sectors:

2.1.1 *Technology Sector*

The technology industry is one of the fastest growing and most dynamic, encompassing everything from computer science and artificial intelligence to cybersecurity and software development. The opportunities in this sector are vast and include professions such as:

- *Software/App Developer:* creates applications and platforms that improve people's daily lives or solve business problems.
- *Artificial Intelligence Engineer:* works with complex algorithms to build intelligent systems that can learn on their own.
- *Cybersecurity expert:* protects digital infrastructures from cyber threats.

Opportunity: It is an ever-expanding sector, which requires problem-solving skills, critical thinking and constant updating of technical skills.

2.1.2 *Healthcare Sector*

Health has always been at the center of society, and this sector offers a wide variety of professions ranging from direct patient care to scientific research:

- ***Doctor or nurse:*** provides direct care to patients.
- ***Biomedical researcher:*** develops new medical treatments and technologies.
- ***Radiology or laboratory technician:*** performs tests and diagnostic analyses that are crucial to patient health.

Opportunity: With an aging population and the constant development of new medical technologies, the healthcare sector is expanding, with an increasing demand for qualified professionals.

2.1.3 *Financial Sector*

The world of finance plays a crucial role in the economic support of companies and individuals. Some of the most popular professions in this sector are:
- ***Financial analyst:*** provides advice on investments and financial strategies.
- ***Accountant:*** Manages business and personal finances to ensure accurate management of resources.
- ***Fintech Expert:*** combines finance and technology to create innovative financial services, such as cryptocurrencies and payment apps.

Opportunities: Innovations such as cryptocurrencies, blockchain and fintech platforms have transformed this sector, making it increasingly dynamic and technologically advanced.

2.1.4 *Creative and Media Sector*

For those with a creative streak, the world of art, media and design offers careers that allow you to express your talent and imagination:

- ***Graphic designer:*** creates visual images to communicate ideas and messages through various mediums.
- ***Digital Content Producer:*** develops and publishes content for online platforms such as YouTube or Instagram.
- ***Writer:*** Specializes in fiction, nonfiction, or marketing content for various industries.

Opportunity: With the growth of digital media and social networks, creative professions are rapidly evolving, opening up new opportunities for freelancers and digital entrepreneurs.

2.1.5 *Educational Sector*

Education remains one of the noblest and most important sectors, with the potential to make a huge difference in people's lives:

- ***Teacher:*** guides and inspires students in their educational journey.

- ***E-learning expert:*** creates digital educational platforms that enable distance learning.
- ***Professional Coach:*** helps people develop skills to improve their job performance.

Opportunities: With the increasing demand for online training, e-learning and distance learning related professions are booming.

2.2 *Analysis of market trends and new professions*

The job market is constantly evolving and in recent years there have been drastic changes, accelerated by technology and new global needs. Let's see the main trends that are redefining the professional landscape.

2.2.1 *Digitization*

Digitalization has transformed virtually every industry, creating new opportunities and professions. From remote work to e-commerce, the world is increasingly connected through digital platforms. Some emerging professions include:

- ***Digital Marketing Specialist:*** manages online advertising campaigns, using data to optimize results.
- ***Data Analyst:*** analyzes large amounts of data to draw actionable conclusions for improving business strategies.

- *UX/UI Expert:* focuses on the user experience and interface of digital applications.

Impact: Digitalization has increased the demand for technological skills in sectors that previously did not require them, making it crucial to continuously update one's digital skills.

2.2.2 *Automation and Artificial Intelligence (AI)*

Automation and AI are radically changing the way we work, reducing the need for some repetitive tasks, but creating new, more complex professions. Some of the new professions linked to this transformation include:

- *Automation Engineer:* Designs and implements automated systems to improve business efficiency.
- *Machine learning specialist:* develops algorithms that enable machines to learn from data without explicit programming.

Impact: While some traditional professions may be disappearing, demand for technical and creative roles is increasing, opening up opportunities in growing sectors.

2.2.3 *Sustainability and Green Economy*

Another important trend is the growing environmental awareness and the transition to a sustainable economy. This is creating new professions in fields such as renewable energy and environmental management:

- ***Expert in renewable energy:*** deals with the development and implementation of clean energy technologies, such as solar and wind.

- ***Corporate Sustainability Consultant:*** helps companies reduce their environmental impact and develop sustainable practices.

Impact: With increasing environmental regulations and changing consumer expectations, sustainability has become a priority for many companies, creating a growing demand for experts in this field.

Conclusion

The world of careers is bigger and more diverse than you might imagine, offering endless possibilities for those willing to explore. Whether you're interested in technology, creativity, finance, or sustainability, there's an industry waiting for you. Understanding emerging trends like digitalization, automation, and sustainability will help you make informed choices and prepare for a career full of opportunities.

Chapter 3: How to Find Your Passion

Introduction

Finding your passion is a personal and profound journey. Many find themselves wondering what their true purpose in life is or what truly makes them happy. This chapter is dedicated to providing you with practical strategies for identifying what you are passionate about, with the goal of moving you closer to a career that not only meets your needs, but excites you every day. We'll explore techniques to discover your passions, such as journaling, mind mapping, and informational interviews, along with visualization and brainstorming exercises to help you imagine the future you want.

3.1 *Practical Strategies to Identify What You're Really Passionate About*

The first step to finding your passion is to put into practice some techniques and methods that help you explore your natural inclinations. Here are some tools that you can use to start this journey:

3.1.1 *Journaling*

The ***Journaling,* or writing in a personal *diary*** , is one of the most powerful tools for self-exploration. Freely writing your daily reflections allows you to organize your thoughts and notice recurring patterns and interests. It can help you identify activities, situations, or people that make you happy or inspire you.

How to Journal to Find Your Passion:
- Spend 10-15 minutes every day free-writing, focusing on your emotions and what gave you energy or left you dissatisfied.
- Focus on past experiences that made you feel accomplished or excited.
- *Ask yourself* : " When do I feel completely immersed and happy?" or "What would I do even if I wasn't getting paid?"

Over time, as you reread your reflections, you may notice common themes that will guide you toward your passions.

3.1.3 *Informational interviews*
Another effective way to explore your passions is to speak directly with people who work in fields that interest you.

Informational interviews allow you to learn more about different professions and to understand if a certain field might interest you.

How to Conduct an Informational Interview:
- * Identify people who work in areas of interest to you (you can find them on LinkedIn or through your personal network).
- * Ask them if they would be available to talk about their work, the challenges and satisfactions they encounter.
- *During the interview, ask questions like: "What are you most passionate about your job?", "What skills or talents are needed?" and "How did you discover your passion for this industry?"

This will give you a real, tangible idea of what it might be like to work in those fields and whether they might align with your interests and values.

3.2 *Visualization and brainstorming exercises*

In addition to practical techniques like journaling or interviewing, visualization exercises and brainstorming can help you imagine your ideal future and generate ideas for a career you're passionate about.

Brainstorming is a creative technique in which you freely generate ideas on a topic without immediately judging them, with the aim of finding solutions or inspiration. It helps to explore many possibilities and stimulate the imagination.

3.2.1 *Guided visualization of the ideal future*

Visualization is a powerful technique that allows you to "see" in your mind the future you desire.

It's one particularly effective tool when it comes to understanding what makes you happy and where you would like to be in a few years.

Visualization exercise:

- * Find a quiet place and sit comfortably.
- *Close your eyes and imagine yourself in five years. Where are you? In which city or environment? How is your work day organized?
- *Imagine your work routine: what do you do every day? Who do you work with? What kind of projects do you follow?
- *Visualize how you feel at the end of a work day. Are you satisfied, enthusiastic, stimulated?

This exercise will help you identify key characteristics of a career you would be passionate about, such as the type of work environment, the type of activities, and the interaction with other people.

3.2.2 *Brainstorming possible careers*

Brainstorming is a creative technique for generating ideas without limits. You don't have to worry about how realistic the ideas you generate are at this stage: the goal is to explore all the possible careers that might excite you.

How to Brainstorm Effectively:
- *Take a sheet of paper or open a digital document.
- *Set a timer for 10-15 minutes and write down every career idea that comes to mind, even the most outlandish or unusual ones.
- *Once your time is up, review your list and identify the ideas that seem most intriguing or resonate with your passions and skills.
- *For each of your most promising ideas, ask yourself: "What attracts me to this career? What personal values or interests does it fulfill?"

This technique will help you explore possibilities you hadn't previously considered, opening your mind to new career paths.

3.3 *Practical activities to identify your passions*

Here are some practical activities you can do to further deepen your passion research:

- *Online Passion Tests:* There are various online tests that can help you identify areas of professional interest based on your personality and preferences.

- *Career Experiments:* Try spending time on small projects or volunteer work in areas that interest you. For example, if you are interested in design, try creating a small graphic design project. These experiments will give you a solid idea of what you enjoy doing.

- *Keep track of emotions:* Every day, make a list of the activities that have given you the most energy and satisfaction, along with those that have frustrated or bored you. This will allow you to notice patterns and trends in what excites you.

Conclusion

Discovering your passion is a journey that takes time, exploration, and reflection. With techniques like journaling, mind mapping, and informational interviews, you can begin to build a greater awareness of what makes you happy and fulfilled. Visualization and brainstorming exercises will then help you imagine your ideal future and generate ideas for potential careers. By following these steps, you'll be well on your way to finding a career that not only excites you, but that truly reflects who you are and what you love to do.

Chapter 4: Build Your Ideal Path

Introduction

Once you have discovered your passion and identified the industry or profession that excites you, the next step is to build a clear and concrete path to reach your goals. Defining a vision for the future is essential, but to make it a reality, you need to set well-structured goals. In this chapter, I will walk you through the process of defining your short- and long-term goals, using the SMART method, one of the most effective techniques for setting and achieving your goals.

4.1 *Why is it important to set clear goals?*

Setting clear goals gives you direction and a concrete plan of action. Goals act as a beacon that guides your decisions and helps you stay motivated, especially in times of uncertainty or difficulty. Without goals, it's easy to get lost or wander without a clear direction. On the other hand, with well-defined goals, you can measure your progress and adjust your path if necessary.

Short term vs long term

The objectives can be divided into:

- ***Short-term goals:*** These are smaller goals that can be achieved over a short period of time, usually within a few months or a year. These goals allow you to make gradual progress and keep your motivation high.

- ***Long-term goals:*** These are goals that take years to achieve. They are tied to your larger vision and define the end result you want to achieve in your career or personal life.

4.2 *The SMART method for setting goals*

The SMART method is one of the most popular for defining clear and effective goals. This acronym represents five criteria that make goals more achievable and concrete:

- ***Specific:*** A vague goal can confuse you and make it difficult to know where to start. Goals should be clear and detailed.
- ***Measurable:*** To understand if you are making progress, you need to be able to measure the results.
- ***Attainable:*** The goal must be realistic and achievable, based on your resources and capabilities.
- ***Realistic:*** The goal must be aligned with your passions, values, and desires.

- *Timed:* There must be a clear deadline, which gives you a time horizon to reach the goal.

4.2.1 *Specific*

A specific goal must answer questions like: **Who? What? Where? When? Why?** For example, instead of saying *"I want to improve my digital skills"*, A specific goal might be *"I want to get certified in digital marketing within six months."*

Helpful questions to make a goal specific:
- *What exactly do I want to achieve?*
- *Why is it important to me?*
- *Who is involved?*
- *What resources or tools are needed to achieve it?*

4.2.2 *Measurable*

Making a goal measurable allows you to track your progress and evaluate whether you're on the right track. This way, you can celebrate small successes along the way, which will help keep you motivated.

For example, a measurable goal might be: *"Study for 2 hours a day"* or *"Complete 5 online courses in the next quarter."*

Helpful questions to make a goal measurable:
- How can I know if I have achieved my goal?
- What metrics will I use to measure success?

4.2.3 Reachable

It is important that goals are realistic and achievable based on your current resources and skills. A goal should be challenging but not impossible, otherwise you risk feeling frustrated or abandoning your path.

For example, if you work full time and have other commitments, it may not be realistic to expect to earn a degree in one year. A more attainable goal might be to complete one or two night courses per semester.

Helpful questions to make a goal achievable:
- Do I have the resources and capabilities to achieve this goal?
- If not, what additional resources do I need?

4.2.4 Realistic - Relevant

A goal should align with your values and aspirations. It should have meaning to you and contribute directly to your professional or personal journey. If a goal isn't *relevant* to you, you'll easily lose motivation.

For example, if your dream is to work in graphic design, getting a certification in accounting may not be *relevant* to your path.

Helpful questions to make a goal realistic:
- Is this goal important to me?
- How does it fit into my career or life plan?

4.2.5 *Timed*
Finally, every goal should have a clear deadline. Without a deadline, you risk procrastinating. Having a timeline helps you stay focused and better plan the steps needed to reach your goal.

For example, a time-bound goal might be "Complete a web programming course by the deadline."

Helpful questions to make a goal timed:
- By when do I want to achieve this goal?
- What intermediate stops do I need to complete along the way?

4.3 *Set short- and long-term goals*

Now that you understand the SMART method, it's time to put the theory into practice by setting both short-term and long-term goals.

4.3.1 *Short-term goals*

Short-term goals serve as small steps toward your larger goals. They should be achievable in a few months or a year and help you progressively build the skills and experience needed to reach your more ambitious goals.

Examples of short-term goals:

- Complete an online course in a field of interest within three months.
- Create a portfolio of five projects within six months.
- Network with at least five industry professionals within a month.

These small steps allow you to see tangible progress in the short term and keep you motivated along the way.

4.3.2 *Long-term goals*

Long-term goals represent your larger, more ambitious vision. These goals take more time and planning to achieve, but setting them gives you a clear direction for the future.

Examples of long-term goals:

- Work as a full-time freelance designer within five years.

- *Achieve a leadership position in the digital marketing industry within three years.*
- *Start your own consulting business within ten years.*

These goals help you stay focused on the big picture and evaluate how your short-term goals connect to your long-term vision.

4.4 *How to monitor progress and adapt the path*

Once you have established your SMART goals, it is essential to monitor your progress and review your goals regularly. milestones. Here are some strategies to ensure you stay on track:

- *Periodic Review:* Set deadlines to regularly review your progress (monthly or quarterly). Evaluate what you have accomplished and what needs adjustment.
- *Flexibility:* Goals can change over time. If you find that a direction no longer suits you, don't hesitate to change it. Adjust your goals as you gain new experiences and skills.
- *Celebrate successes:* Every time you reach a goal, big or small, take a moment to celebrate. This will strengthen your motivation and give you the energy to take on new challenges.

Conclusion

This way, you will be able to stay motivated, adapt to challenges and celebrate every step forward. The SMART method will help you stay focused and measure results, making your journey more structured and rewarding. With commitment and consistency, your goals will turn into concrete successes, bringing you ever closer to achieving your ideal path.

Chapter 5: Overcome Challenges and Achieve Success

Introduction

On the path to achieving your goals and building a career that you will enjoy, you will inevitably encounter challenges. Stress, fear of failure, and procrastination are common obstacles, but they can be overcome if you address them with the right strategies. In this chapter, I will provide you with practical techniques to manage these difficulties and guide you in creating a winning mindset, which is essential for maintaining motivation and focus. Through success stories and inspiring quotes, you will discover that overcoming obstacles is not only possible, but can become an essential part of your path to success.

5.1 *Strategies for managing stress, fear of failure and procrastination*

5.1.1 *How to manage stress*

Stress is the body's natural response to challenging situations. While a little stress can even motivate you, Too much stress can be crippling. The key is to develop techniques that help you reduce and manage it effectively.

Practical strategies for managing stress:
- ***Breathing Techniques:*** When you feel overwhelmed, try diaphragmatic breathing or the ***4-7-8 technique (inhale for 4 seconds, hold for 7 seconds, exhale for 8 seconds).*** These exercises calm the nervous system and immediately reduce anxiety levels.

- ***Regular exercise:*** Activities such as yoga, jogging, or even a simple walk help release endorphins, which improve mood and reduce stress.

- ***Planning and time management:*** Organize your activities by breaking tasks into small, manageable steps and prioritize them. Using tools like to-do lists or calendars can help you avoid feeling overwhelmed by your workload.

- *Take breaks:* Short breaks during the workday are essential to recharge and maintain high productivity. Techniques such as the *Pomodoro method (25 minutes of work followed by a 5-minute break)* can be helpful.

5.1.2 *Dealing with the fear of failure*

Fear of failure is one of the most common obstacles and can keep you from taking initiative or trying new things.
However, failure is an inevitable part of the learning and growth process. Accepting that failure does not mean that you are failing as a person, but rather that you are learning, is the first step in overcoming this fear.

Tips to overcome the fear of failure:
- *Reframe failure:* See failure not as an obstacle, but as an opportunity to learn and improve. Every mistake brings you closer to success. *As Thomas Edison said, "I haven't failed. I've just found 10,000 ways that don't work."*

- *Take small steps:* Break your goals into smaller, more attainable milestones. This will reduce the pressure and build confidence as you go.

- *Visualize Success:* Take a few minutes each day to imagine yourself achieving your goals. This technique helps you focus on what you want to achieve. rather than what you fear.

- *Accept uncertainty:* No one can predict with accuracy what will happen in the future. Learning to live with some degree of uncertainty will make you more resilient and help you make decisions even when you are not completely in control.

5.1.3 *Overcoming procrastination*

Procrastination may seem like a trivial problem, but it can seriously slow down your path to success. It often stems from fear, insecurity, or mental overload. Overcoming it means finding a balance between discipline and mental well-being.

Practical methods to overcome procrastination:
- *The 2-Minute Technique:* If you feel overwhelmed by a task, try starting with something very small that you can complete in 2 minutes. Once you get started, you'll be more likely to continue.
- *Break down tasks:* A goal that is too big can be intimidating. Break down the work into smaller, less daunting tasks. A list of short, achievable tasks is easier to manage.

- *Make your goals public:* Sharing your progress with friends or colleagues can increase your sense of accountability and push you to finish what you start.

"do the worst first" rule : If you have a task you don't want to tackle, start with that. Once you get past the difficulty, everything else will seem easier.

5.2 Winning Mindset to Achieve Your Goals

In addition to overcoming practical obstacles, having a positive and resilient mindset is crucial to long-term success. How you approach challenges and opportunities largely determines how far you can go. A winning mindset focuses not only on the end result, but on the process and learning along the way.

5.2.1 What is a winning mindset?

The *Winning Mindset* It is based on some fundamental beliefs:
- *Growth instead of fixation:* People with a *growth mindset* believe that their abilities and intelligence can be developed through effort, learning, and perseverance. They do not see challenges as threats, but as opportunities to improve. In contrast, those with a *fixed mindset* tend to avoid challenges for fear of failure.

- *Resilience:* The ability to recover quickly from difficulties is an essential quality for anyone who wants to be successful. Resilience allows you to get up after every failure and learn from every experience.

- *Optimism and positivity:* Having a positive attitude does not mean ignoring difficulties, but facing them with the belief that every problem has a solution.

5.2.2 *How to develop a positive mindset*

Here are some techniques to develop and maintain a positive mindset:

- *Accept difficulties as part of the process:*
There is no growth without challenges. Change your perspective and see difficulties as opportunities to improve.
- *Surround yourself with positive people:* The people you spend time with influence your mindset. Try to surround yourself with people who support you and motivate you to grow.
- *Practice gratitude:* Every day, take some time to reflect on what you are grateful for. This will help you maintain a positive mindset even when faced with difficulties.

- ***Learn to say no:*** The ability to set limits will allow you to focus on what is truly important, avoiding wasting energy on activities that do not bring you closer to your goals.

5.2.3 *Success Stories and Inspirational Quotes*

Many successful people have faced challenges similar to the ones you are experiencing. Their experiences prove that failure is never the end, but rather a stage in the journey to success.

JK Rowling's Story: Before "Harry Potter" became a worldwide phenomenon, JK Rowling received numerous rejections from publishers. Her perseverance, despite the difficulties, eventually led to the publication of one of the most popular books of all time. Rowling said: " ***It is impossible to live without failing at something, unless you live so cautiously that you have not lived at all – in which case, you have failed anyway.***"

Inspirational quote by ***Michael Jordan:*** Jordan is considered one of the greatest basketball players in history, but he also failed many times. He said: " ***I have failed over and over again in my life and that is why I have succeeded.***"

Story : Before the success of *Tesla and SpaceX*, Elon Musk has faced numerous financial and technical failures. He has persevered, believing strongly in his vision of a sustainable and technological future, demonstrating how resilience and long-term vision are essential to success.

Conclusion

Overcoming challenges is part of the journey to success. With the right strategies to manage stress, fear of failure and procrastination, and by developing a winning and resilient mindset, you will be able to face any obstacle. Success stories prove that every difficulty can be transformed into an opportunity

Chapter 6: Helpful Tools and Resources

Introduction

On your journey to building a passionate and fulfilling career, having access to the right tools and helpful resources can make a big difference. Whether you're looking to improve your skills, explore new opportunities, or stay up-to-date on industry trends, there are many resources available to support you in achieving your goals. In this chapter, you'll find a collection of books, websites, online courses, and helpful tools that can help you on your professional growth journey.

6.1 *Books for personal and professional growth*

Books remain one of the most valuable resources for gaining in-depth knowledge and new perspectives. Here is a selection of essential texts to develop your skills, meet the challenges of work, and build a career you are passionate about.

6.1.1 Books on mindset and personal growth

- Mindset: Changing Your Mindset for Success by *Carol S. Dweck* : A classic on growth mindset, this book will help you understand how your beliefs affect your ability to learn and improve.

- The Power of Now by Eckhart Tolle : This book explores the importance of living in the present and approaching challenges with awareness. Perfect for those who want to reduce stress and develop a positive mindset.

- Atomic Habits by James Clear : A fundamental text for those who want to improve their daily habits and achieve extraordinary results through small, consistent changes over time.

6.1.2 *Books on career success and leadership*

- Stephen Covey's 7 Habits of Highly Effective People : Covey offers a systematic, principled approach to achieving professional and personal success, with a focus on productivity, leadership, and interpersonal relationships.

- Leaders Eat Last by Simon Sinek: A book that explores leadership from a servant perspective, explaining how to create a work environment where people can thrive.

- Purple Cow by Seth Godin : A classic for those who want to stand out in their field. Godin discusses the importance of being extraordinary and standing out in a crowded market.

6.1.3 *Books to explore passions and choose a career*
- *Find Your Why" by Simon Sinek:* This book will guide you through a process of discovering your "why"—what you're truly passionate about—and helping you choose a career that reflects your values.

- *Designing Your Life* by *Bill Burnett and Dave Evans:* Using the principles of design thinking, the authors help you build a career and life that are meaningful and fulfilling.

6.2 *Useful websites and platforms*

The digital world offers a wealth of resources for those who want to improve their skills and explore new careers. Here are some of the most useful websites for career growth.

6.2.1 *Online course platforms*
- *Coursera ([coursera.org](https://www.coursera.org))* : Offers online courses from universities and companies around the world on topics ranging from technology to science to soft skills. Many courses are free with the possibility of obtaining certificates for a fee.

- *Udemy ([udemy.com](https://www.udemy.com)):* An online course platform with thousands of courses on a wide range of topics, including marketing, programming, photography, and personal growth.

- ***LinkedIn Learning ([linkedin.com/learning](https://www.linkedin.com/learning):*** Offers professional courses focused on technical and soft skills essential for the modern workplace. The platform is integrated with LinkedIn, making it easy to showcase your newly acquired skills on your profile.

- ***edX ([edx.org](https://www.edx.org)):*** An online education platform with courses from prestigious institutions such as Harvard and MIT. Covers advanced academic topics and professional skills.

6.2.2 *Networking Tools and Career Opportunities*

- ***LinkedIn ([linkedin.com](https://www.linkedin.com)*** : The world's largest professional social network, ideal for building and maintaining professional relationships, searching for job opportunities, and sharing your career path.

- ***Meetup ([meetup.com](https://www.meetup.com):*** This platform allows you to find local or online events where you can connect with people who share your interests, whether to grow professionally or explore new passions.

6.2.3 *Freelance work platforms and projects*

- *Fiverr ([fiverr.com](https://www.fiverr.com):* A global marketplace for freelancers, where you can offer or buy services in areas such as graphic design, digital marketing, writing, and programming.

- **Upwork ([upwork.com](https://www.upwork.com)):** Another freelancing platform that lets you work on projects around the world, building a portfolio and building a career remotely.

6.3 Courses and certifications for professional growth

Continuing education is essential to staying competitive in the modern workplace. Here are some of the best options for courses and certifications that can enhance your resume and open up new opportunities.

6.3.1 Technical skills courses

- *Google Career Certificates (grow.google:* Offered by Google, these courses provide certifications in fields such as IT Support, Project Management, and Data Analysis. They are highly regarded by employers and allow you to access growing jobs.

-*MicrosoftLearn (docs.microsoft.com/learn* :

Offers courses and certifications on Microsoft tools and technologies, such as Azure and Power BI, ideal for those who want to work in the IT and technology sector.

6.3.2 *Soft skills and leadership courses*
- ***Dale Carnegie Training ([dalecarnegie.com](https://www.dalecarnegie.com):*** A resource for developing communication, leadership and management skills. Dale Carnegie courses are known to improve the ability to build relationships and manage teamwork effectively.
- ***Toastmasters International ([toastmasters.org](https://www.toastmasters.org):*** An organization that helps improve public speaking and leadership skills through local clubs and meetings.

6.4 *Productivity Apps and Tools*

In addition to courses and learning resources, there are a number of apps and tools that can improve your productivity, organization, and personal growth.

6.4.1 *Time and project management tools*

- *Trello (trello.com):* A visual board-based project management tool that's perfect for organizing your work and tracking your progress in a simple, intuitive way.

- *Todoist (todoist.com):* One of the most popular to-do list apps, it lets you create task lists, set due dates, and track your daily and weekly priorities.

- *Asana (asana.com):* A powerful project management tool, perfect for teams and freelancers who want to collaborate and keep track of all ongoing tasks.

6.4.2 *Tools for personal growth*

- *Headspace ([headspace.com](https://www.headspace.com)):* A meditation app that helps you reduce stress and improve mental well-being, which is essential for maintaining a positive and productive mindset at work.

- *Evernote (evernote.com* : An app for taking notes and organizing ideas. It is especially useful for those working on complex projects or need a place to collect thoughts and inspiration.

Conclusion

Having access to the right tools and resources is essential to building a career that you're passionate about and fulfilled. From inspiring books to online learning platforms, productivity apps to training courses, these resources will help you grow professionally and achieve your goals. Investing in your learning and personal growth is not only a way to improve your skills, but also to discover new

Chapter 7: How to create an effective CV

Creating an effective curriculum vitae (CV) is essential to stand out in the job market. work. Here is a step-by-step guide to writing a CV that will grab employers' attention:

1. Choose the right format

There are several different CV formats, but the most common are:

- *Chronological:* Ideal if you have a solid work experience. List the most recent experiences first.

- *Functional:* focuses on skills rather than work history, great for career changers or those with gaps in their work.

- *Combined:* combines the strengths of the chronological and functional CV.

2. Enter your contact information

Contact information must be clear and up-to-date:

- *Name and surname*

- *Professional email address*

- *Phone number*

- *LinkedIn or portfolio (if relevant)*

Make sure they are easy to find at the top of your CV.

3. Write a professional objective or personal profile

Start with a short paragraph describing who you are, what your goals are, and what you can offer. This is the time to immediately capture the employer's attention.

- *Professional objective:* Highlight what you are looking for and your ambitions.

- *Personal profile:* an overview of your experiences, key skills and successes.

4. Describe your work experiences

List your work experience in reverse chronological order (most recent first). For each position, include:

- *Position title*

- *Company name and location*

- *Period of employment (start and end month and year)*

- *Description of responsibilities and achievements (use short sentences and concrete results)*

Suggestions:

- *Use action verbs (e.g., "managed," "coordinated," "developed").*

- *If possible, quantify the results (e.g., "20% increase in sales").*

5. Include key skills

Create a section dedicated to skills that are relevant to the job you are applying for. Skills can be divided into:

-*Hard skills:* specific technical skills *(e.g. programming, project management).*

-*Transversal skills:* e.g. leadership, communication, problem-solving.

6. Add academic training

Please include your educational qualifications, listing them from most recent to least recent:

- *Title name (e.g. Bachelor's, Master's)*

- *Institute and city*

- *Period of attendance*

- *Any votes, mentions or awards (optional)*

7. Enter any certifications or training courses

Add any certifications, courses, or workshops that are relevant to the job you want. This is especially helpful if you have acquired new skills or want to strengthen existing ones.

8. *Languages*

If you know more than one language, create a specific section and indicate your level of proficiency (native, advanced, intermediate, basic).

9. *Extracurricular projects or experiences*

If you have worked on personal projects, volunteer work, or extracurricular experiences, you can include them if they are relevant to the job you are applying for.

10. *Customize your CV for each application*

It is important to tailor your CV to the position you are applying for. Carefully review the job ad and include keywords that are present in the job description.

11. *Check and optimize the layout*

- *Use a clean and uncluttered design with a well-organized structure.*

- *Keep your CV to one or two pages maximum (unless you have a very long career).*

- USA *bullet points (bullet points)* to make reading easier and keep focus on the most important elements.

- *Choose a readable font (such as Arial, Calibri, or Times New Roman).*

12. *Proofreading and revision*

Before sending your CV, check for typos, grammar or formatting errors. It may be helpful to have someone else review it.

By following these steps, you will be able to create a well-structured resume that will appeal to employers.

Chapter 8: How to Face a Job Interview

1. *Learning about the company* is a crucial step in preparing for an interview. Knowing the company in depth allows you to demonstrate genuine interest and connect your skills to the organization's goals.

Why is it so important to learn about the company?

Demonstrate Interest: Show the interviewer that you have taken the time to learn about the company and that you are genuinely interested in the position.

Allows you to personalize your answers: You can connect your experiences and skills to the company's projects and values, making your answers more relevant and memorable.

Helps you understand the company culture: Understanding the company's values and culture helps you assess whether the work environment is a good fit for you and prepares you for questions about your compatibility with the company.

Increase your security: Knowing the company well will make you feel more prepared and confident during the interview.

Where to find information:

Company website: The website is the most comprehensive source of information about the company. Look for the "About Us," "Our History," "Values," and "Careers" sections.

Social profiles: Corporate social media can provide more informal insights into company culture and ongoing projects.

News and Articles: Search for recent company news on search engines and news sites.

LinkedIn: Your company's LinkedIn profile can provide information about employees, open positions, and current projects.

Talking to former employees: If you know someone who has worked or works in the company, ask about your experience.

What information to look for:

Industry: What industry does the company operate in? Who are the main competitors?

Mission and vision: What are the company's values and goals?

Products and services: What products or services does the company offer? Who are its main customers?

Company Culture: What is the work environment like? How are employees valued?

Recent Projects: What are the most important projects the company is working on?

Challenges and opportunities: What are the main challenges and opportunities the company is facing?

How to use this information:

Connect your experiences: Show how your previous work experiences have prepared you to meet the company's challenges.

Expressing Interest: Show that you know the company and are enthusiastic about its operations.

Ask relevant questions: Prepare questions that demonstrate your interest and knowledge of the company.

Example question:

"I saw on your website that you are launching a new product in the [industry name] industry. How do you think this initiative will impact the role of [role you are applying for]?"

In conclusion, taking the time to learn about the company is an investment that will allow you to make a better impression during the interview and increase your chances of success.

Salary negotiation

Negotiating salary is a delicate but important part of the process. Here's how to do it successfully:

- *Do market research:* Research the average salary for the position and industry, using sites like ***Glassdoor or Payscale.***
- *Evaluate the overall package:* Consider not just salary, but also benefits, vacation, work flexibility, etc.
- *Wait for the right moment:* Avoid talking about salary early in the interview. Wait for the company to make an offer.

- *Communicate your value:* Explain how your skills and experience add value to the company.

- *Don't be afraid to ask:* If the initial offer is low, don't hesitate to make a counteroffer, but always be polite and professional.

2. Preparing answers to the most common questions is a fundamental step to face an interview with confidence and success. Here is how you can develop this point further:

Preparing Answers: Your Secret Weapon

Having clear and concise answers to the most frequently asked questions will allow you to face the interview with greater peace of mind and convey an image of professionalism and preparation.

Why prepare answers in advance?

Increase Confidence: Knowing what to say in advance will make you feel more confident.

Improve communication: You will have time to organize your thoughts and express your ideas clearly and concisely.

Show interest: Prepared and relevant answers demonstrate that you care about the position.

Manage Anxiety: Knowing what to say will help reduce your nervousness.

What questions should you prepare?

In addition to the questions you've already mentioned, here are some other common questions you may encounter:

Why should we hire you? What are your career goals?
Describe a professional success of yours.
Describe a professional challenge of yours.
How do you manage stress?
How do you work in a team?
What is your current salary?
How to prepare answers:
Customize your responses: Tailor your answers to the specific position and company you are applying for.
Be concise: Avoid going on too long, get straight to the point.
Use concrete examples: Support your answers with specific examples from your experience.
Highlight your strengths: Highlight the skills and experiences that make you the ideal candidate.
Be positive : Even when you talk about your weaknesses, try to turn them into opportunities for growth.
Example answer to the question "Tell me about yourself":
"I am [your name] and I am [your age]. I have [number] years of experience in the [industry] industry and have worked at several companies, including [name of companies]. My main skills are [list your main skills]. I am a [describe your personal characteristics, for example: motivated, proactive, results-oriented] person. I am particularly interested in this position

because [explain why you are interested in the position and the company].

Additional tips:

Use the STAR method: When describing an experience, use the STAR method (Situation, Task, Action, Result).

Practice out loud: Try answering questions out loud to get used to expressing your ideas clearly and fluently.

Ask for feedback: Ask a friend or family member to listen to you and give you feedback.

In conclusion*,* preparing answers to the most common questions is an investment of time that will bring you great benefits. It will allow you to face the interview with greater confidence and increase your chances of success.

3. Role-playing an interview is a great way to prepare yourself and reduce anxiety. Here's how you can build on this:

Mock Interview: The Key to Success

Playing an interview with a friend or family member is like a dress rehearsal before a performance. It allows you to familiarize yourself with the dynamics of the interview, practice your answers, and receive constructive feedback.

Why simulate an interview?

Increase Confidence: By simulating the interview, you will feel more prepared and confident.

Improve your answers: You will have the opportunity to refine your answers to common questions.

Manage Anxiety: Practicing an interview helps you overcome nervousness and feel more comfortable.

Get feedback: A friend or family member can give you advice on how to improve your communication and body language.

How to simulate an interview:

Choose the right person: Choose someone who knows you well and is willing to give you honest feedback.

Create a realistic environment: Try to recreate an environment similar to that of the real interview.

Prepare your questions: Ask your friend or family member to ask you the most common questions that might be asked during an interview.

Time the time: Simulate the actual length of the interview to get used to managing your time.

Ask for feedback: After the simulation, ask your friend or family member to give you feedback on your performance.

What to ask during feedback:

How did I communicate? Was I clear and concise?

How did I manage my body language? Did I maintain eye contact? Did I speak in an appropriate tone of voice?

How did I answer the questions? Were my answers relevant and complete?

What impression did I make? Did I seem confident? Motivated?

Additional tips:

Record the simulation: If you have the opportunity, record the simulation to review it later and analyze your strengths and weaknesses.

Simulate different scenarios: Try answering different questions and unexpected situations.

Be open to feedback: Accept your friend or family member's advice with humility and try to improve yourself.

In conclusion, simulating an interview is a very useful exercise to prepare yourself as best as possible. It allows you to gain more confidence, improve your communication skills and increase your chances of success.

4. Clothing is a key element in communicating your professionalism during an interview. Here's how you can develop this point:

Clothing: Your First Message

The way you dress is your first business card. Choosing appropriate clothing is a way to show respect for the company and the role you are applying for.

Why is it important to take care of your appearance?

First impression: The way you dress significantly affects the first impression you make on the interviewer.

Professionalism: Proper and well-groomed clothing communicates seriousness and professionalism.

Congruence with the role: By choosing an appropriate outfit, you demonstrate that you understand the characteristics of the role and the company.

Confidence in yourself: Dressing well can boost your self-esteem and make you feel more confident.

How to choose the right clothing:

Learn about the company culture: Find out if the company has a formal or informal dress code.

Consider the role: Choose clothing that is appropriate for the position you are applying for.

Opt for a clean and tidy look: Clothes must be clean, ironed and well matched.

Avoid excesses: Don't wear clothes that are too tight, low-cut or too casual.

Choose neutral colors: Dark colors like black, navy blue, or gray are generally considered more professional.

Additional tips:

Take care of the details: Pay attention to details like clean shoes, neat hair, and manicured nails.

Bring a jacket with you: It may be helpful to have a jacket to suit a more formal setting.

Avoid overly intense perfumes: Too strong a perfume could annoy your interlocutor.

Be yourself: Your clothing should reflect your personality, but always maintain a professional tone.

In conclusion*,* clothing is an important aspect to consider when preparing for an interview. By choosing an appropriate outfit, you will project a professional image and increase your chances of success.

5. The importance of punctuality during an interview cannot be overstated. Here's how you can further develop this point:

Punctuality: A Sign of Respect and Professionalism

Arriving on time for an interview is a clear sign that you respect other people's time and demonstrates your professionalism. Being late, even by a few minutes, can leave a negative impression and hurt your chances of success.

Why is it so important to be punctual?

It conveys professionalism: Show that you are a reliable person and that you respect your commitments.

Create a positive first impression: A punctual candidate is perceived as organized and detail-oriented.

Show interest: By arriving on time, you show that you care about the interview and that you are genuinely interested in the position.

It allows you to start the interview in a calm manner: If you arrive early, you have time to relax and prepare yourself mentally.

How to make sure you are on time:

Plan your route in advance: Use a sat nav or map app to find your route and estimate travel times.

Consider the traffic: Find out about traffic conditions and plan your trip accordingly.

Plan for unforeseen events: Consider factors such as public transport delays, roadworks or difficulty finding parking.

Arrive a little early: Arriving 10-15 minutes early is ideal. It will allow you to relax and get familiar with the environment.

Verify the address: Make sure you have the exact address of the interview location and how to get there.

What to do if you still have to delay:

Notify me immediately: If you expect a delay, please notify your contact as soon as possible.

Sincerely apologize: Briefly explain the reason for the delay and apologize for the inconvenience caused.

Be concise: Avoid giving too many details and focus on making an effort to get to the interview location as soon as possible.

In conclusion, punctuality is a fundamental aspect of any interview. By arriving on time, you demonstrate that you are a reliable and professional person, thus increasing your chances of making a good impression and getting the job you want.

6. Having all the materials you need for an interview is essential to convey an image of professionalism and organization. Here's how you can develop this point further:

Bring Everything You Need: Prepare for Success

Having all the documents required for an interview on hand is a small gesture that can make a big difference. It not only shows your organization and attention to detail, but it also allows you to be prepared to answer any questions the interviewer may have.

What to bring:

Curriculum vitae: Make sure it is up to date and matches the information you provided in your application. Bring several copies with you.

Reference List: Include the names, companies, roles and contact details of people willing to provide a reference for you.

Portfolio (if required): If you work in creative fields, bring a portfolio showing your previous work.

Notepad and pen: To take notes during the interview and write down any questions.

Identification: It may be required to access company offices.

Other Certifications: Any certifications or diplomas that may be relevant to the position.

Why it is important to bring everything you need:

Demonstrate organization: An organized candidate is more reliable and professional.

It makes you feel more confident: Having everything at your fingertips saves you time searching for important documents.

It allows you to answer any question: If the interviewer asks you to elaborate on a point in your resume, you can do so immediately.

Make a good impression: A prepared and organized candidate leaves a great impression.

Additional tips:

Organize a Folder: Use a folder to keep everything organized.

Check the requirements: Before the interview, double check which documents are specifically required.

Bring an extra copy: In case you forget something, having an extra copy will save you.

In conclusion, bringing all the necessary materials is a small gesture that can make a big difference. Do not underestimate the importance of this simple action, which can contribute significantly to your success.

7. Showing interest is essential to making a good impression during an interview and increasing your chances of success. Here's how you can develop this point further:

Showing Interest: The Key to Success

In addition to managing emotions and communicating effectively, it is crucial ***to demonstrate genuine interest*** in the role and the company. This will not only set you apart from other candidates, but will also allow you to gain valuable insights and evaluate whether the opportunity is a good fit for you.

How to show interest:

Do thorough research on the company : Before the interview, learn about the company's history, values, products/services, and recent successes. This will allow you to ask targeted questions and demonstrate that you've done your homework.

Connect your experiences to the company's needs: Explain how your skills and previous experience can contribute to the achievement of the company's goals.

Ask relevant questions: Show your interest by asking for details about the role, responsibilities, work dynamics, growth opportunities, and company culture.

Listen carefully: Pay attention to what the interviewer tells you and ask probing questions.

Express enthusiasm: Show that you are truly motivated and want to be part of the team.

Examples of relevant questions:

About the role:

"What are the main responsibilities of this position?"

"What are the most significant challenges I will face?"

"What are the main goals I should achieve in the first year?"

About the company:

"What are the company's core values?"

"How do you see the company evolving in the coming years?"

"What are the opportunities for professional growth within the company?"

About the team:

"How is the team I will be working with structured?"

"What are the work dynamics within the team?"

Why it's important to ask questions:

Demonstrate Interest: Show that you have done your homework and are genuinely interested in the position.

Get valuable insights: You can clarify doubts and get a more complete picture of the opportunity.

You differentiate yourself from other candidates: You demonstrate proactivity and curiosity.

Evaluate whether the company is a good fit for you: Understand whether the company values and culture align with your expectations.

Additional tips:

Prepare a list of questions: This will help you not to forget anything during the interview.

Adapt the questions to the context: Customize your questions based on the information you've gathered about the company and role.

Be authentic: Questions should be sincere and reflect your genuine interest.

In conclusion, showing interest is a key element to making a good impression during an interview. By preparing in advance, asking pertinent questions and showing enthusiasm, you will increase your chances of success and finding a job that you are happy with.

8. Managing emotions during an interview is essential to conveying confidence and competence. Here's how you can develop this point further:

Managing Emotions: A Step Towards Success

It's completely natural to feel a little nervous before or during an interview. Your adrenaline is flowing, your heart is beating a little faster... but don't despair! With a little preparation and the right strategies, you can transform that nervousness into positive energy.

Why is it important to manage emotions?

Transmit security: A calm, controlled attitude communicates confidence in your abilities.

Improve communication: When you are relaxed, you are able to express your ideas better.

You create a positive impression: A confident, confident candidate is more memorable.

How to manage nervousness?

Take a deep breath: Diaphragmatic breathing helps calm the body and mind.

Visualize Success: Imagine the interview going well, this will help you feel more confident.

Prepare answers to common questions: Having some answers in mind will give you more confidence.

Arrive early: Avoid last-minute stress and find a quiet place to relax.

Focus on the present: Avoid thinking about the past or the future, focus on the present moment.

Speak slowly and clearly: This will give you time to organize your thoughts.

Smile: A smile conveys positivity and makes you feel more relaxed.

Additional tips:

Take care of yourself: Sleep well the night before, eat a balanced breakfast and wear comfortable clothes.

Observe your body language: Maintain an upright and open posture, avoid crossing your arms or legs.

Listen carefully to the questions: Before answering, make sure you understand the question.

Be yourself: Authenticity is always appreciated.

Remember: It's normal to be nervous, but with the right strategies, you can turn that nervousness into an opportunity to shine.

9. Here are some options for rephrasing the advice on interview manners, with a more detailed touch:

Option 1: Emphasis on body language

Get off to a good start. A firm handshake, a genuine smile, and direct eye contact are the first steps to making a good impression. These simple nonverbal gestures convey confidence, professionalism, and friendliness, creating a positive atmosphere from the beginning of the interview.

Option 2: Focus on the importance of first impressions

First impressions count. A warm greeting, with a firm handshake and a smile, is your business card. These small gestures, apparently trivial, can make the difference, transmitting confidence in your abilities and positively predisposing the interlocutor towards you.

Option 3: Linking Body Language and Effective Communication

Communicate even without speaking. Body language is powerful: a firm handshake, a sincere smile, and direct eye contact are essential elements of effective communication. These gestures not only convey confidence and professionalism, but also help you create empathy with the interlocutor, facilitating the exchange of information.

Additional tips:

Maintain an upright and open posture: Communicates security and interest.

Listen actively: Show attention to what the speaker is saying.

Modulate your voice: A clear, toned voice conveys energy and professionalism.

Avoid excessive gesticulation: It could distract the interlocutor.

Why is it important to follow these instructions?

You create a positive first impression: Essential to generate interest in your profile.

Convey confidence and professionalism: Qualities that are highly appreciated in the workplace.

Facilitate communication: An open and positive body language encourages the exchange of information.

You demonstrate interest and involvement: Show that you are attentive and focused on the conversation.

In summary, These simple nonverbal gestures are a powerful tool to communicate your personality and skills. Invest a little time in refining your body language and you will see that it will make a difference during your next interview.

10. *During the interview:*

Shake hands firmly and look the person in the eye.

Repeat his name to show attention.

Express your sincere thanks for taking the time and giving you the opportunity to learn about the company.

Summarize briefly the key points of the conversation that most interested you.

Reiterate your enthusiasm for the position and for the company.

Ask when you can expect a response .

Example sentence:

"Thank you very much for your time and for this interesting conversation. I was particularly impressed by your focus on innovation and the opportunity to work on such challenging projects. I remain very interested in the position and am very excited to contribute to the success of your team. Could you tell me what the next steps are?"

After the interview:

Send *a thank you email within 24 hours* .

Personalize the message: mention specific details from the interview to demonstrate your interest and attention.

Reiterate your strengths and how they can be useful to the company.

Confirm your enthusiasm for the position and for the company.

Make yourself available for any further interviews or questions.

Email structure:

Object: Thank you for the interview - [Position Title] - [Your Name]

Greetings: Dear [Name of Recruiter],

First paragraph: Thank them for the interview and reiterate your interest.

Second paragraph: Mention specific details from the interview and tie your skills to the company's needs.

Third paragraph: Reiterate your availability and conclude with a formal greeting.

Email example:

> Dear [Name of the selector],
>
> I am writing to thank you again for taking the time to interview me yesterday for the position of [Job Title]. I was very impressed with your description of the [Project Name] project and believe that my experiences in [Area of Expertise] can be an added value to your team.
>
> As I mentioned, I am particularly passionate about [Topic of Interest] and have always admired the way your company addresses industry challenges. I am confident that my skills in [Key

Competencies] would allow me to contribute significantly to achieving the team's goals.

Thank you again for your consideration and I remain at your complete disposal for any further information.

Best regards,

[Your name] [Your telephone number]
[Your email]

Additional tips:
Adjust your tone and language to the type of company and location.
Use formal, professional language .
Please carefully correct any grammatical errors .
Send the email from a professional email address .
Why is it important to send a thank you email?
It sets you apart from other candidates .
Demonstrate your interest and professionalism .
It gives you the opportunity to reiterate the key points of the interview .
It may open the door to further discussions .

Chapter 9: How to Manage Networking

Introduction

Networking is one of the most important skills in the professional world. Building and maintaining a network of contacts can open doors to new opportunities, foster professional growth, and provide support and mentorship. In this chapter, we explore key strategies for managing networking effectively.

1. *Define Your Goals*

Before you start building your network, it is essential to be clear about your professional goals. Ask yourself:

> *What are your short and long term goals?*
> *In which sectors or areas do you want to grow?*
> *What kind of contacts could help you achieve these goals?*

2. *Attend Networking Events*

Attending networking events is a great way to meet new professionals. Some suggestions include:

> ***Conferences and Seminars*** *:* Attend events relevant to your industry.
> ***Industry Events*** *:* Trade shows, exhibitions and industry meetings are great opportunities to make new acquaintances.

> ***Corporate Events*** : Attend events organized by your company or partner companies.

3. Use Professional Social Media

Professional social media, such as LinkedIn, are powerful tools for building and maintaining relationships. Some tips include:

> ***Create a Professional Profile*** : Make sure your profile is complete, up-to-date and professional.
> ***Connect with Other Professionals*** : Send connection requests to colleagues, clients, and other professionals in your industry.
> ***Participate in Discussion Groups*** : Join relevant discussion groups and participate in conversations to increase your visibility.

4. Offer Value

Providing value to others is essential to building strong professional relationships. Some tips include:

> ***Share Knowledge and Skills*** : Offer your help and skills to support others.
> ***Provide Helpful Resources*** : Share articles, books, and other resources that may be useful to your contacts.
> ***Be a Good Listener*** : Listen carefully to the needs and concerns of others and try to offer solutions.

5. Keep in Touch

Keeping in touch with your contacts is essential to maintaining strong professional relationships. Some tips include:

> ***Send Follow-Up Messages*** : After meeting someone at an event, send a follow-up message to keep in touch.

Arrange Regular Meetups *:* Schedule regular meetups, such as lunches or coffees, to keep the relationship alive.
Use Social Media *:* Interact with your contacts on social media by commenting and sharing their posts.

6. *Be Authentic and Genuine*

Authenticity is key in networking. Try to be yourself and build relationships based on trust and mutual respect. Authentic relationships are those that last over time and bring the greatest benefits.

Conclusion

Networking takes time and effort, but the benefits can be enormous. By following these strategies, you will be able to build and maintain a strong and successful professional network.

Chapter 10: How to Stay Motivated and Achieve Your Goals:

In summary

How to Stay Motivated and Achieve Your Goals

Staying motivated and achieving your long-term goals can seem like a challenge, but with the right techniques and strategies, you can stay motivated and achieve your dreams. Here are some effective techniques to help you stay motivated and achieve your goals:

1. Set Clear and Realistic Goals

> ***Specific:*** Goals should be clear and well-defined. For example, instead of saying *"I want to get fit ,"* specify *"I want to lose 5 kg in three months."*
> ***Measurable:*** Make sure your progress can be measured. This will help you see how close you are to achieving your goal.
> ***Attainable:*** Goals should be realistic and attainable. Avoid setting goals that are too ambitious and may discourage you.
> ***Relevant:*** Goals must be important to you and aligned with your values and desires.

Timed: Set a deadline for your goals. This will help you stay focused and work with a sense of urgency.

2. Create an Action Plan

Small, Manageable Steps: Break your goals into small, manageable steps. This will make the process less intimidating and more achievable.
Prioritize: Identify the most important tasks and focus on them. Avoid dispersing your energy on too many things at once.
Track Progress: Track your progress regularly. This will help you stay motivated and make any adjustments to your plan.

3. *Stay Motivated*

Visualization: Imagine yourself achieving your goals. Visualization can increase your motivation and strengthen your determination.
Rewards: Reward yourself for small successes along the way. This will give you a sense of accomplishment and motivate you to continue.
Face Challenges: Accept that there will be obstacles along the way. Prepare yourself mentally to face and overcome them.

4. *Seek Support*

Share Your Goals: Talk about your goals with friends, family, or colleagues. Their support can be a source of motivation and encouragement.
Find a Mentor: A mentor can offer you valuable advice and guide you on your journey.
Support Groups: Join groups or communities that share your goals. Mutual support can be very motivating.

5. Maintain a Positive Mindset

Self-discipline: Cultivate self-discipline and resilience. Remember that perseverance is the key to achieving your goals.

Learn from Mistakes: See mistakes as learning opportunities. Every failure is a step towards success.

Stay Flexible: Be willing to change your plans if necessary. Flexibility will help you adapt to changes and stay on track.

6. Review and Adjust Your Goals

Periodic Evaluation: Review your goals regularly to ensure they are still relevant and achievable.

Adapt: Don't be afraid to adjust your goals if circumstances change. The important thing is to stay focused on your path.

www.ingramcontent.com/pod-product-compliance
Lightning Source LLC
Chambersburg PA
CBHW071044240526
45471CB00014B/562